My Very Own Bible

Stories retold by
Betty Fletcher

ILLUSTRATED BY LOU POLICE

CANDLE
BOOKS

Published in the UK by Candle Books 1993.
Reprinted 1994, 1995, 1996, 1998, 1999 twice,
2000, 2001, 2002, 2003
Distributed by STL, PO Box 300, Carlisle
CA3 0QS

Worldwide co-edition arranged by
Angus Hudson Ltd., Concorde House,
Grenville Place, Mill Hill, London NW7 3SA

Tel: +44 20 8959 3668
Fax: +44 20 8959 3678
E-mail: coed@angushudson.com

Printed in Singapore

CONTENTS

Old Testament Stories

New Testament Stories

Introduction

The Bible is divided into two parts. The first part is called the Old Testament. The Old Testament is full of exciting adventures about people who lived before Jesus was born.

The New Testament tells us about Jesus. The stories show how Jesus helped people and how He taught them about God the Father.

The most important thing we learn from the Bible is that God loves us. He sent Jesus to die on the cross so that if we believe in Him, we can become part of God's family and live with Him forever.

Old
Testament
Stories

GOD MAKES
OUR WORLD

In the beginning God made the world. It was very dark. God said, "Let there be light." And there was!

God made the sun and the moon and the stars and put them just where He wanted them. He made plants and animals, birds and fish, to make our world beautiful. Then He made a man and a woman.

Do you know their names?

The man was Adam and the woman was Eve.

It took God six days to make our world. When He was finished He said, "This is very, very good." And He rested on the seventh day.

Genesis Chapters 1 and 2

A TALK IN
THE GARDEN

God gave Adam and Eve the Garden of Eden for their home. He said, "You may eat anything that grows in the garden except the fruit of the special tree."

While Eve was looking at the special tree, a snake spoke to her. "God won't really mind if you eat from the special tree. You don't have to obey Him."

Eve listened to the snake. She looked at the pretty fruit. Oh, how she wanted to try it! Finally she ate it. Adam ate it too.

God came to talk with them.

"Because you haven't obeyed," God said, "you must leave the beautiful garden."

Genesis Chapters 2 and 3

NOAH BUILDS
A BIG BOAT

Time passed, and the earth was filled with people who were not good. This made God very sad. He decided to wash His world clean.

One man was good. His name was Noah. God told Noah to build a big boat.

People laughed at Noah. They didn't believe God would send a flood, but Noah believed. He filled his boat with animals of every kind.

It began to rain. It rained for forty days and forty nights. Only Noah's big boat was safe.

After the flood God put a rainbow in the sky. He promised Noah: "I will never flood the whole earth again."

Genesis Chapters 6 to 8

A COAT
FOR JOSEPH

Jacob had many children, but Joseph was his favorite. Jacob loved his young son so much that he gave him a wonderful coat, a coat of many colors.

Joseph's brothers were jealous. They sold Joseph to traders who were going to Egypt. His brothers told their father that Joseph had been killed by a wild animal.

Joseph became a great man in Egypt, but he missed his family. When he heard they had no food to eat, he asked them to come live with him in Egypt. His father was surprised. He thought Joseph was dead. His brothers were surprised too. They were glad that Joseph forgave them!

Genesis Chapters 37 to 45

A PRINCESS
FINDS A SON

After Joseph died, God's people became slaves in the country of Egypt. Their lives were very hard. One day the king of Egypt said, "Kill every baby boy that is born to a slave mother."

But baby Moses' mother hid him in a basket. She put the basket in the tall grass by the bank of the river.

One afternoon the king's daughter came to the river to take a bath. She saw the little basket and opened its lid. There was baby Moses! He was crying. The princess felt sorry for Moses. She took him to the palace and made him her son.

Exodus Chapter 2

A PATH
THROUGH THE SEA

When Moses grew up, he left the palace because the king was angry with him. For many years he lived in the desert. One day God talked to Moses.

"Take My people away from Egypt," God said. "I want to give them a new place to live."

Moses obeyed God.

This made the king very angry. He chased Moses to the Red Sea.

Moses pointed over the sea, and the water disappeared down the middle. God's people walked to the other side. The king's army tried to follow, but the water came crashing down on them, and they were drowned.

Exodus Chapter 14

GOD'S
GOOD RULES

God's people traveled through the desert to a mountain called Sinai. God met Moses there on the mountain.

"I want to give My people some rules," God said. "I want to teach them how to live."

God wrote His rules on two tablets of stone and gave them to Moses. Moses carried them down to the people.

We call these rules the Ten Commandments. They teach us to love God, to obey our parents, and not to lie. These rules helped God's people in their long journey to their new land.

They are very good rules, don't you think?

Exodus Chapters 19 and 20

THE WALLS
FALL DOWN

When they reached the land God had promised them, God's people had to fight the people of Jericho. Jericho had thick, high walls.

God showed their leader, Joshua, just what to do.

"March around the city once each day for six days," God said. "On the seventh day, march around the city seven times. Then have the leaders of God's family blow their trumpets. When the trumpets sound, tell the people to shout with all their might."

The seventh day finally came. The people could hardly wait. When the last trumpet sounded everyone gave a great shout, and the walls of Jericho fell down flat.

Joshua Chapters 5 and 6

GOD'S
LITTLE ARMY

God chose a good man named Gideon to be the captain of His army. Before the battle God said to Gideon, "You have too many men. Send most of them home."

God wanted Gideon to trust Him.

"Now give every man who is left a trumpet, and a clay pot with a torch in it," God said.

"What a strange way to fight!" thought Gideon.

Late that night Gideon's little army made a ring around the enemy camp. When Gideon gave the sign they broke their pots and blew their trumpets. The bright lights and noise scared the sleeping soldiers, and they ran away from Gideon's army.

Judges Chapters 6 and 7

SAMSON,
THE STRONG MAN

Samson was very strong. God made Samson strong so he could fight his enemies, the Philistines.

A woman named Delilah tricked Samson into telling her what made him strong. He said, "If you cut my hair I will become weak."

While Samson slept, Delilah cut his hair. She called the Philistines. They poked out Samson's eyes and took him to jail.

Slowly Samson's hair grew back. One day the Philistines brought Samson to their meeting place to make fun of him. Samson prayed, "Lord, make me strong just one more time." Samson pushed hard against the stones that held the building up. And the walls tumbled down on top of the Philistines.

Judges Chapters 13 to 16

RUTH,
THE FRIEND

Naomi and Ruth were good
friends. They lived together after
their husbands died.

Naomi was much older than
Ruth. One day Naomi said, "I want
to live in Bethlehem. It is my
hometown. But this is where you
are from. You stay here."

"I want to go wherever you go,"
Ruth said.

So they went to Bethlehem.
Ruth worked in the fields to get
food to eat. The owner of the field
saw how hard she worked. He said
to her, "I've heard how you left your
own hometown to take care of Naomi.
And I've seen what a good friend
you've been. May God bless you."

Ruth Chapters 1 to 4

GOD
CALLS SAMUEL

When Samuel was a little boy he lived with Eli, a man who loved God. One night Samuel heard a voice calling, "Samuel! Samuel!"

Samuel ran to Eli. "Did you call me?" he asked.

"No. Go back to bed, little one," Eli said.

This happened again...and again. Then Eli realized that the Lord was calling Samuel. "Go back to bed," Eli said, "but this time when you hear the voice, say, 'Speak, Lord. I am listening.'"

This is what Samuel did. After that night God spoke to Samuel many times. Samuel gave the people God's messages. He was called a prophet.

1 Samuel Chapter 3

DAVID
AND GOLIATH

David the shepherd boy had an errand to do! He was going to the battlefield with food for his older brothers.

When he arrived, David saw that the soldiers were filled with fear because of a giant named Goliath.

"Why are you scared?" David asked. "I'm just a shepherd boy, but when a lion comes to eat my sheep, God helps me kill it. And God will help me kill the giant."

David gathered five stones from the river. He hurled one from his slingshot. It hit Goliath in the forehead and the giant fell down on his face. David grabbed Goliath's huge sword and cut off his head.

1 Samuel Chapter 17

GOD'S GIFT
TO SOLOMON

Solomon became the king of Israel when he was very young. One night the Lord came to Solomon in a dream.

"What would you like me to give you?" God asked.

"Lord, I am young. I don't know how to be a good king," Solomon said. "Please make me wise. Help me understand right and wrong."

God was very pleased with Solomon.

"I'm glad you asked to be a good ruler instead of asking for treasure. I will make you the wisest man who ever lived." And that's just what happened.

You can find many of Solomon's wise sayings in the Bible.

1 Kings Chapter 3

The Oil That Wouldn't Stop

A poor woman owed a lot of money. She had to pay or her sons would become slaves. She asked Elisha the prophet to help her.

"What do you have in your house?" Elisha asked.

"Nothing but a small jar of oil," she answered.

"Go borrow all of the pots and jars you can find," said Elisha. "Then pour the oil from your tiny jar into the others."

The woman poured and poured and poured. The oil didn't stop until the last big jar was filled to the top.

The woman sold the oil and paid her debt. She even had money left to live on.

2 Kings Chapter 4

NAAMAN
TAKES A BATH

A man named Naaman also came to Elisha. Naaman was an army captain from another country. He had a very bad sickness called leprosy.

Elisha told Naaman, "Go wash in the Jordan River seven times and you will be well."

This made Naaman very angry. "There are rivers in my own country. I didn't come to take a bath. I came to be healed."

But his servants said, "If Elisha asked you to do something big, wouldn't you do it? Then why not do this little thing?"

So Naaman washed in the river and was made well. He believed in God because God healed him.

2 Kings Chapter 5

GOOD
QUEEN ESTHER

In a faraway country a Jewish girl name Esther married the king. One day Queen Esther's uncle told her that some of the king's men were going to kill the Jews.

"You must speak to the king."

"I can't," said Queen Esther. "I'm afraid."

"You must," said her uncle. "Perhaps God made you queen so that you could save your people!"

Queen Esther prayed, and God gave her an idea. She gave the king a wonderful party. He was so pleased that he let her ask for anything she wanted. She asked the king to help her people, and he did so gladly.

Esther Chapters 1 to 10

THE BURNING
FIERY FURNACE

The king of Babylon made a big gold statue. He told everyone to bow down to it.

Three young men said no.

"I will throw you into the burning fiery furnace if you do not bow to my statue," cried the king angrily.

The king told his men to make the fire hotter and hotter. "Tie them up and throw them in!" he said.

But the fire did not burn them!

The king knew God had saved the young men. He was sorry for what he had done. He made Shadrach, Meshach, and Abednego rulers in his kingdom.

Daniel Chapter 3

DANIEL AND
THE HUNGRY LIONS

When Darius was king, a law was made that anyone who prayed to God would be thrown to the lions. But Daniel would not stop praying.

King Darius loved Daniel, but even the king had to obey the law. He threw Daniel into a deep hole filled with hungry lions. The next morning the king called out, "Daniel, has your God been able to save you?"

Daniel said, "O king, God sent His angel and shut the lions' mouths!" The king was glad. He pulled Daniel out and dropped the men who had made the law into the hole, where the lions ate them up.

Daniel Chapter 6

JONAH AND
THE BIG FISH

One day God said to Jonah, "Go to the city of Nineveh. Tell the people to stop being bad."

Jonah was afraid, so he sailed far away on a ship. But God had a job for Jonah in Nineveh and sent a big storm. When the sailors found out that the storm was Jonah's fault, they threw him overboard.

God sent a big fish to swallow Jonah. It was cold and dark in the fish's belly.

Jonah prayed – he prayed and prayed – for three days. Finally the fish spat him back onto the dry land. Jonah went straight to Nineveh. The people listened to him and started being good.

Jonah Chapters 1 to 4

New Testament Stories

MARY
HAS A BABY

One day an angel named Gabriel came to visit Mary. "You're going to have a baby!" the angel said. "He will be God's Son."

"I will gladly do whatever God asks," Mary said to the angel.

Mary and Joseph, the man she was going to marry, were in Bethlehem when the time came for baby Jesus to be born. All of the hotels were full. The only place they could stay was in a barn.

Mary had her baby there with the donkeys and sheep. She wrapped baby Jesus in a blanket and gently laid Him in a manger filled with hay. How happy she was!

Luke Chapters 1 and 2

THE STAR

In a faraway country, wise men saw a bright star in the sky. They knew the star meant someone special had been born. They wanted to see Him.

They followed the star for many nights. Finally the star stopped at Mary and Joseph's house.

They talked to Mary.

"The child who was born will be a very great man," they said. "We have come to bow down to Him."

Mary brought Jesus out, and the wise men bent very low. They gave Him gold and sweet-smelling gifts.

Then they went back to their own land.

Matthew Chapter 2

A MISSING BOY

When Jesus was twelve, He went to Jerusalem for a holiday with His family and friends.

After the holiday, the big group started home. Mary and Joseph thought Jesus was walking with His friends. But Jesus was missing! Mary and Joseph couldn't find Him anywhere. They hurried back to Jerusalem. They looked all over the city for Jesus. Finally they found Him talking to the teachers in God's house.

"Jesus, you worried us!" Mary said.

"Didn't you know that I would be in My heavenly Father's house?" Jesus asked. Then Jesus went home with Mary and Joseph, and He grew strong and wise.

Luke Chapter 2

THE MAN WHO
ATE GRASSHOPPERS

Jesus had a cousin named John. John lived in the desert and ate grasshoppers and wild honey. People came from all around to hear him teach about God. If they wanted to obey God, John baptized them.

One day Jesus asked to be baptized. When He came up out of the water, John saw a dove come down from heaven and rest on Jesus. This was a sign from God.

John heard God's voice: "This is My Son. I love Him."

"I knew Jesus was my cousin," John thought, "but now I know He is God's Son."

Matthew Chapter 3

FISHERS OF MEN

One day Jesus went for a walk beside the lake. He saw two brothers, Peter and Andrew, throwing their fishing nets into the water.

Jesus called to them, "Come with Me, and I will make you fishers of men." He meant that Peter and Andrew would be His special helpers.

Farther along Jesus saw James and John. Jesus called them. They jumped out of their boat to go with Him too.

Jesus asked twelve men in all to be His helpers. Here are their names: Peter, Andrew, James, another James, John, Matthew, Bartholomew, Judas, Thaddeus, Philip, Simon, and Thomas.

Luke Chapter 5

A HOLE
IN THE ROOF

When people in the town of Capernaum heard that Jesus was coming, they rushed to see Him. A man who could not walk wanted to see Jesus too. But it was so crowded he could not get near.

This man had four friends. They climbed on top of the house where Jesus was teaching and made a big hole in the roof. Then they lowered their friend down right in front of Jesus.

Do you think Jesus was mad? No, He was not. He was happy, and He made the man well. Everyone was amazed to see the lame man walk, and they thanked God.

Mark Chapter 2

JESUS HELPS
A SICK GIRL

Jairus was worried. He had to find Jesus. "Jesus, my little girl is dying," he said when he found Jesus by the lake. "Please come and touch her. I know you can make her well."

On the way a man met them. "Don't bother Jesus anymore," the man said. "Your daughter is dead."

But Jesus turned to the father and said, "Don't be afraid. Just believe in Me."

When they got to the house, Jesus took the girl's hand. "Little girl, it's time to get up," Jesus said. The little girl opened her eyes and got up from her bed. Jesus had made her well.

Mark Chapter 5

JESUS
MAKES SUPPER

There were always lots of people around Jesus. They liked to hear Him talk.

One day Jesus talked until late in the afternoon. It was time for supper!

"Give the people something to eat," Jesus told His helpers.

"We don't have enough food," His helpers said. "One boy has five loaves of bread and two fish, but that's all."

"Bring it here," Jesus said. He thanked God for the bread and began tearing it into big pieces. He kept handing bread and fish to His helpers until they had given food to everyone.

That day Jesus fed five thousand people with two fish and five small loaves of bread.

John Chapter 6

PETER
WALKS ON WATER

After Jesus fed the people He wanted to be alone to pray.

His helpers started rowing their boat across the lake.

The wind started blowing. Whoosh! Whoosh! Whoosh! In the dark, stormy night Jesus walked to His helpers on the water.

They thought He was a ghost.

Peter said, "If it really is you, Lord, tell me to come to you."

Jesus said, "Come." So Peter got out of the boat, stood up on the water, and began to walk toward Jesus. Then he became frightened. He started to sink! But Jesus grabbed his hand and helped him back into the boat.

Matthew Chapter 14

THE GOOD
NEIGHBOUR

Jesus told a story about a man who went on a trip. Along the way robbers beat the traveler and took his clothes.

One of the leaders of God's people saw the hurting man, but he didn't stop to help him. Another man who worked in God's house also saw him. But he left him lying on the road.

A third man came along. He wasn't anyone special. He wasn't even from the same town as the man who was hurt. But he put the man on his donkey and took him to a house where he could get well.

Which man was a good neighbour to the hurting man?

Luke Chapter 10

THE LOST SON
COMES HOME

One day a boy said, "Father,
I don't want to live here anymore.
Please give me my share of every-
thing you own."

The son went away and foolishly
spent all his money. The only job he
could find was feeding pigs.

Finally the tired, hungry boy
went home. He hadn't been a good
son, but perhaps his father would
let him be a servant.

When his father saw him coming
he ran to meet him. He was so
happy! He kissed his son and threw
a big party for him. "I thought I had
lost you," the father said, "but here
you are. Welcome home!"

Luke Chapter 15

HUGS
FROM JESUS

Jesus loved children. One day as He was talking to a big crowd of people, a group of parents brought their children to Him. They wanted Jesus to bless them. But Jesus' helpers shooed them away. "Don't bother Jesus," they said. "Can't you see He's busy?"

Jesus saw what His helpers were doing. He was angry. "Don't tell the children to go away! Let them come to Me. Everyone who goes to heaven must believe in Me just as these little ones do."

Then the children ran to Jesus. He gathered them into His arms and blessed them.

Mark Chapter 10

BLIND
BARTIMAEUS

Bartimaeus was blind. Every day he sat by the road and asked people for money to buy food.

One day he heard the sound of many feet on the road. "Who's coming?" he asked.

"Jesus," the people said.

Bartimaeus had heard that Jesus could make people well. He called out, "Jesus! Jesus!" The people told him to be quiet, but he shouted even louder, "Jesus!"

Jesus heard him calling. "What do you want Me to do for you?" he asked.

"I want to see," said Bartimaeus.

"I will make you see because you believe in Me," said Jesus.

At that very moment Bartimaeus saw Jesus. He wasn't blind anymore!

Luke Chapter 18

A LITTLE MAN
CLIMBS A TREE

Zaccheus was late. Now he'd never get to see Jesus. He was too short to see over all of the tall people.

Zaccheus thought, "I will run ahead and climb that big sycamore tree. Then I will be able to watch Jesus go by."

It worked! But Jesus didn't go by Zaccheus. He stopped right beneath the sycamore tree.

"Zaccheus, come down," Jesus called to him. "I want to spend the day with you."

"With me? You want to spend the day with me?"

Zaccheus was so excited he nearly fell out of the tree. Jesus wanted to be Zaccheus' friend! Jesus changed Zaccheus' life with His love.

Luke Chapter 19

THE POOR
WOMAN'S GIFT

Some people dressed in fine clothes went to God's house to give gifts of money. A woman dressed in poor clothes also went to give her gift. She gave only two pennies. That wasn't very much.

Jesus was watching. He talked to His helpers. "See the two pennies that poor woman put into the money box? Those two pennies mean more to God than all of the money the rich people put in. Those people had lots of money. They will hardly miss what they gave. But this poor woman gave everything she had."

Jesus was happy that the woman trusted God to take care of her.

Luke Chapter 21

A Sad Day

Jesus came to earth to do something very special. He came to take the punishment for all of the bad things we have done.

Jesus was in a garden praying when the time came. Soldiers took Him to the judges. The judges hated Jesus because He said He was the Son of God. They called Jesus a liar and said He must die.

The soldiers took Him to the top of a hill and nailed Him to a wooden cross. When He died, they buried Him in a cave and rolled a big stone across the doorway.

Jesus' friends were very sad. But God had a surprise for them!

Mark Chapters 14 and 15

WHERE
IS JESUS?

Sunday came, and Mary went to the cave where Jesus was buried. The big stone had been rolled away.

"Oh no! Someone has taken Him away!"

She ran to tell Jesus' friends. When she came back later, she heard a voice behind her.

"Mary," the voice said.

Mary turned to see who was calling her. It was Jesus. He wasn't dead anymore. He was *alive*!

That night some of Jesus' friends met in a room with the doors closed. Suddenly Jesus was with them. He talked to them for a long time. They were glad Jesus was alive again. It was the most wonderful thing that had ever happened.

John Chapter 20

DOUBTING
THOMAS

Thomas wasn't with the other friends when they saw Jesus.

"I don't believe He's alive," Thomas said. "I want to see the holes in His hands and touch the place where the soldiers stabbed Him."

Thomas had to wait a week before Jesus came to see His friends again. This time Thomas was there. "Put your finger into the holes in My hands," Jesus said. "Touch the place in My side."

Then Thomas believed.

"You are happy now because you have seen Me. But people who don't see Me and still believe will be even happier than you."

Jesus was talking about you and me.

John Chapter 20

SONGS IN
THE NIGHT

Bang! The doors of the jail clanged shut. Paul and Silas had been put in jail for telling people about Jesus.

Late in the cold, dark night Paul and Silas started praying and singing. The other men listened.

Suddenly an earthquake shook the jail and all the doors opened wide. The jailer was scared. He thought everyone would run away and he would be punished.

"Don't worry," Paul called to him, "we're still here."

The jailer knew God had sent the earthquake. He asked how he could know God. Paul and Silas told him to believe in Jesus. The jailer and his whole family believed in Jesus that very night.

Acts Chapter 16

WHAT WILL
HEAVEN BE LIKE?

The very best thing about heaven is that we will be able to see God and Jesus. We will talk with them. We will sing with them. We will live with them in a city made of gold and sparkling with jewels of green and blue and yellow and red. A beautiful river will run through the city. It will be a bright and happy place.

Everyone who loves and follows Jesus will be in heaven. No one will be sad or sick, and no one will ever, ever die. God will love us and we will love Him and be with Him forever.

Revelation Chapters 21 and 22